This book belongs to:

To my son Francesco ♥

Author: Serena Lane Ferrari (www.serenalaneferrari.com)
Illustrator: Giorgia Vallicelli (www.giorgiavallicelliart.com)
Published by Save the Planet Books

First Printing, 2019
ISBN: 979-12-200-5110-1

Saving Tally

An Adventure into the Great Pacific Plastic Patch

Written by
Serena Lane Ferrari

Illustrated by
Giorgia Vallicelli

Tally Turtle once saved a young lobster from a fisherman's trap. They became best friends and now they live with Granny Turtle and other strange creatures in the great Pacific Ocean.

At the break of dawn, Grandma Turtle wakes Tally up and says,

"Tally, now that you are growing up,
I think the time has come for you
to explore the Coral Reef with Ara.
You can set off on an adventure together."

Tally twists and jiggles like a mermaid.

"But watch out, Tally," says Grandma,
"Beware of the plastic patch. It's the most dangerous place to be."

"Is it more dangerous than a stinging **jellyfish**?" asks Tally.
"Yes, my darling, it is," says Grandma.

"Is it more dangerous than the giant jaws of a **shark**?"
"Yes, my darling, it is much more
dangerous than the giant jaws of a shark."

"Is it more dangerous than the
terrible speedboats?"

"Yes, my darling, it is even more dangerous than the terrible **speedboats**."

"Okay, Granny," says Tally as she swims away
as fast as a shooting star with Ara clinging to her shell.

After gliding and sliding, they arrive at the rainforest of the sea: Coral Reef.

They flip in and out of the sparkling corals. They paddle with seahorses and dangle amongst schools of colourful fish.

Tally watches crabs playing hide-and-seek on the rocks.

She spots a funny creature with one eye peeping in the dark.

"I'm having an adventure!" says Tally,
not taking the time to slow down.

NOT that way!" shouts Ara chasing Tally.

Tally dives and pops in and out of the water,
like a dancing ballerina.

She travels along the reef until...

... She is lost.

Tally spots some lovely bright colours
floating beneath the waves.

Strange shapes gently gliding,
some come to rest on the ocean floor.

She moves towards the patch feeling **hypnotised**.

"**THE PLASTIC PATCH!**" screams Ara,
scuttling off to hide under a clump of sand.

Tally twists and spins surrounded by plastic parts,
trying to escape.

She is trapped in a plastic bag!

She curls and twirls.
She loops and dips.
But the plastic bag wraps her even tighter!
She shivers.

Tally screams, "**Save me! I'm caught in here!**"

As quick as a flash, Ara flings herself towards her friend.

Raising her powerful claws, she swoops on the plastic bag.
She rips and scratches, slashes and shreds.

The bag is torn to pieces.

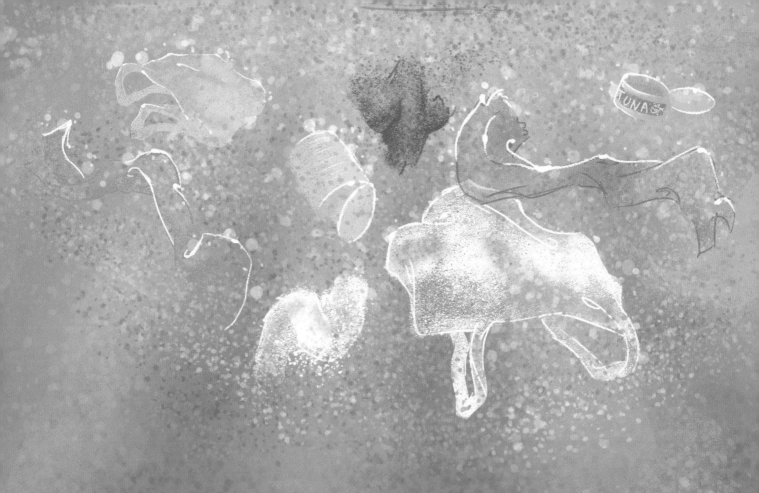

Tally ducks under the mass of floating
plastic and the two friends **swim away.**

Past the stingy jellyfish.
Past the grinning shark and his giant jaws.
Past the terrible speedboats.

They crawl up the beach and gaze back at the waves.

"Thank you Ara!
If it weren't for your courage, I wouldn't have been saved.
Let's tell everyone how dangerous it is to throw plastic
into our ocean."

Tally and Ara, with a flipper and a claw, write on the shore.

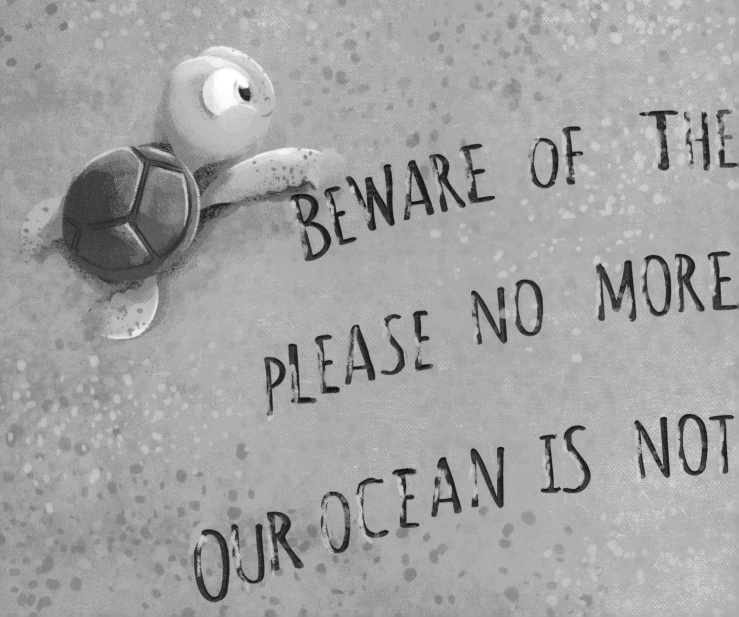

BEWARE OF THE

PLEASE NO MORE

OUR OCEAN IS NOT

PLASTIC PATCH
LITTER IN THE OCEAN
A GARBAGE CAN

GREAT PACIFIC GARBAGE PATCH

46% OF THE TOTAL MASS IS MADE OF DISCARDED FISHING GEAR

99% OF EVERYTHING IS PLASTIC

1.6 MILLION KM²
994.193 MILLION MILES

1.8 TRILLION PIECES OF PLASTIC

80.000 TONS OF GARBAGE

San Francisco

Hawaii

Mexico

8% MICROPLASTICS
0.05CM > 0.5CM

13% MESOPLASTICS
0.5CM > 5CM

26% MACROPLASTICS
5CM > 50CM

53% MEGAPLASTICS
> 50 CM

GARBAGE CONCENTRATION
Kilograms per square kilometers

200 miles

0.01   0.1   1   10   100

What can we do about ocean plastic pollution?

Everyone can do something to reduce the amount of plastic that enters the ocean.

Here are six ways you can make a difference.

1. Reduce your use of single-use plastics (say no to straws)

2. Use reusable water bottles

3. Avoid products containing microbeads

4. Use reusable shopping bags

5. Participate in a beach or river cleanup

   and..

6. Spread the word!

Help make others aware of the problem.

Tell your family and friends about how they can be part of the solution.

From the Author

I write books for young children that have the **future of our planet** at their heart. I passionately believe that children are our last chance to improve our ecosystems, find solutions to major climate problems, and save the planet.

I also believe in the importance of **reading to children** from an early age, and hope that my books engage children (and parents!) and inspire them to believe in a better future.

I love hearing from readers, and welcome you to **interact with me** on facebook (www.facebook.com/SerenaLaneFerrari) or to **contact me** at serenalaneferrari@gmail.com

Would you mind taking a few seconds to leave a review of my book? It's important because **your opinion** helps people make better decisions.

Thank you!

Serena Lane Ferrari

The Hidden Spaceship

When Amelia and Noah stumble across a spaceship, an out-of-this-world adventure begins. The friends have a very special mission - **to help save the Earth's ecosystem**. They must go on a daunting journey on another planet, find a treasure chest, and complete their quest. What secret does the treasure chest hold?